T0339676

SENTIMENTS

*

Poetry

Jackson Matimba

Mwanaka Media and Publishing Pvt Ltd,
Chitungwiza Zimbabwe

*

Creativity, Wisdom and Beauty

Publisher:

Mmap

Mwanaka Media and Publishing Pvt Ltd

24 Svosve Road, Zengeza 1

Chitungwiza Zimbabwe

mwanaka@yahoo.com

https//mwanakamediaandpublishing.weebly.com

Distributed in and outside N. America by African Books Collective

orders@africanbookscollective.com

www.africanbookscollective.com

ISBN: 978-0-7974-9550-0

EAN: 9780797495500

DISCLAIMER

All views expressed in this publication are those of the author and do not necessarily reflect the views of *Mmap*.

Table of Contents

INTRODUCTION

SENTIMENTS is a compiled volume of 41 poems. The poems speak of feelings that we have already experienced and some of which we will have to come across in our different lives. The poems are full of emotions that comes out of simple things that happen in every single minute in our daily living. We see the sun coming up every morning, we see the wind stirring the tree leaves; flowers are blossoming everywhere around us all the time. Feelings of falling in love, feelings of losing a loved one as a result of death. We relive these experiences through the poems in this book.

Due to the fact that the word 'SENTIMENTS' is such a broad term itself, the poetry in this collection covers a variety of themes and emotions; coupled with originality, simplicity, distinctiveness and skill. Although the poems are mostly centred on the emotions of the human being, there is also some focus on his/her judgement, attitude, belief, opinion, idea, thought, and view; and his reaction to all these traits of behaviour.

These are friendly poems in that they easily mix with the feelings already dwelling in our hearts and effortlessly captures the imagination of the reader. They plainly tell of your story as a person practically living in this beautiful, delightful and sometimes troubled world. When you are reading this book you will never feel lonesome, but you are encouraged where you are not brave enough. Above all, the poems endeavours to open up all our eyes and hearts to the little things of nature which we always overlook, yet these little things play some special roles in our hearts that even our learned physicians oftentimes are not able to match.

SENTIMENTS is poetry in its simplest form, yet so deep in its richness, flavour and structures. Every poem is written and left in its natural and pure state. If you want to see the natural and pure state of the water from a river you should go up to the mountains where the source of the river is located. Such a natural form tapped from this book is only equivalent to the nectar that a bee goes down inside of a bottle flower to collect; or a stone of gold that a miner goes deep underground to fetch. The bulk of the lines carry direct messages and they are easily linked to enable the New Reader to be carried away by the winds of poetry which in true essence; are the lines, verses and stanzas from the first to the last wording, in an easy and gentle manner.

Every poem comes from a source of some feelings. Such are the general thoughts of the mind being triggered by the emotions from the heart. But these sentiments are not to be strong as to the point of being sentimental. This brings us to another point in the book which asks that should there always be a limit to the ways that we react to all issues which affect us, and to all things that we see happening in the world? But do we know the appropriate levels of our emotions in some of the situations already stated above? Or should there be an appropriate level.

Sentiments cannot be fully explained or examined in their behaviour. We may try to do so, but we will always leave something to question and answer. To me it's kind of a zone in us which we cannot fully control and comprehend. I will not agree less with *Tendai Rinos Mwanaka* as he wrote in his poem,

CATHEDRAL OF DETOURS:

> *"It's kind of a zone*
> *Blood zone, life zone, knowledge*
> *Zone, grinding zone*
> *Danger zone, separate zones,*
> *gaps sewed together*
> *with strings zones*
> *Life's pendulum swinging*
> *between the two zones*
> *Life and death's zones…"*

In this book we are approaching and tackling the issues of sentiments in a totally poetic way, because it is so hard and nearly impractical and misleading to do it as an essay, in an academic way. Actually poetry writing and sentiments are really two inseparable cookies. You can't write poetry without first stirring up some kind of emotion. The mind alone cannot write a good poem, it also needs the [inner instinctive sense and feeling] to make the poem a living form of literature.

Poems

SENTIMENTS OF MIGRATION

I am packing my bags
To go back to Africa
I am packing my coal skin
And my flat nose
And my afro kinky hair;
Packing everything away
To go back to Africa;
To find a home for my black skin.

I have packed my kinky hair
And my so called brown eyes
I am packing my thick accent
And packing up my carbon lips
Packing my Black theology
To go back to Africa,
To find an answer for my lost religion;
To seek a home for my flat nose;
And to find a home for my racial heritage.

I am sneaking by the night
Slinking like a dog
To go back to Africa.....
I am leaving by the back door
In a peaceful & humble manner
I am leaving by the old galleons
Docked where once,

My ancestors once landed in chains;
Packing to go back to Africa;
To find a home for my black poetry.

I cannot run away from my Negro skin
By bleaching it with light creams;
I cannot fix up my flatly framed nose;
I cannot stretch my kinky hair;
I cannot bash in my overhanging brows
So I have to pack my bags,
Packing my bags of a torn culture;
Packing to go back to Africa
To find a home for my black ideology.

I must be packing my black children
Packing everything black in my suitcases
My monkey face, packing!
My bushy paws, packing!
My long tails, packing!
Packing my overhanging brows
And my shiny black smiles
To go back to Africa
To seek a home for my inborn image.

I am packing & packing my pain;
all my daily disappointments, packing.
The scars all over my body, packing.
Packing all my frustrations.

3

My broken dreams are all packed;
I am packing them away
Packing everything with deep & silent pride
To sail thither to Africa;
To find a home for my African sepia skin;
To find a home for my sons & daughters.

NOT WILLING

I am not willing
To fly with you over the cirrus clouds
Because I fear;
If my wings are broken
You may leave me falling to the ground.

I am not sure;
To walk with you in the drizzled rain
Behold my fear;
If I get wet
You might leave me for one who is dry.

I am not willing
To go with you on a treasure hunt
Because I'm scared
If we find the treasure
You might stab me on the back.

I'm not keen,
To swim with you across the Red sea
Because my dread;
When the waves get strong
You might drop me along the precarious way.

I am not willing

To go with you to the Anglo-Saxon war
Behold my guess;
If I get wounded
You might leave me to die on the battlefield.

I am not willing
To carry the pregnancy of our prince
Because my worry;
If a girl child is born
He might turn me back to my father's house.

I'm not willing
To exchange with you the marriage vows
To mark my fear;
If I get old
You may leave me for one who is young.

I'm not confident to walk
With you through the veldt fire
Because I know if I am burnt
You might not put out the flames consuming me.

#FALLING FROM ABOVE

Falling....
falling......
falling.........
                   I am falling in love
& I am thinking,

                          As I am falling;
                 Will it be a hard or a soft landing?
             But that will depend on my own emotions.
                       I am falling
                         Am falling
& falling;

            Falling through a mass of the bright stars
       Spinning across the millions of the blinding sun's rays
           Falling without control, falling head over heels
                  I am falling in love
               Falling like a broken bird
 falling towards the ground
  Falling in the drizzle, the rain & snow
                  Falling like a hunting kite
I am falling through the hollow & white moon
                   Falling like an astronaut
                 Enjoying the moment's ride
             Falling without humps and bumps
                     I am falling

As falling…..
Falling for the first time, falling @ the right moment
Without a scream, am falling

I am falling silently.
I can't sleep, because;
I am falling in the middle of the night
I am falling in love

I am smiling all the way down

I don't know what to do
I am confused as I fall face down
Falling dismally in love

I am dizzy
I am flying
I am happy
I don't care
I am surprised
Even gravity cannot restrain me

Now that I am falling like a tumbling plane
Accidentally falling in love

I am restless

My breasts are itching
I am moist everywhere
Sweating & freezing at the same time
But I am really feeling so excited.
I can't eat, I can't sit + I can't see
Because I am falling so fast
Through the empty spac
Falling in love with him

I am falling
Falling from the rooftop of my feelings
Falling from the ladder of my sanity
Falling from the grasp of my footing
Falling in love with her
She is falling
He is falling
We hold hands
And continue falling
Without knowing where I may be landing
But I am not afraid

Because;

I am falling in love's arms.

THE POEM

I write a passionate poem
For my beautiful lover,
Whom I wish
I could wed this summer.

I sing a compassionate poem
For my ailing mother;
She is battling cancer in the hospital.

I dedicate a poetry verse
To my beloved Jesus Christ;
He died for me on the Cross.

I write a warm & sweet poem
For my little children;
That I left
At home when I joined the war.

Today I sing a sad poem
For my beloved pantry
That is being plundered
Day and night
By the powerful & greedy few.

She is writing a bleeding verse
With drops of tears from a rural pen
As she await for her children
That went away many years ago.

I murmur a poetry prayer
For my small family every evening
So that God may see them through
The things that we cannot see.

I pen a poetry book
For Africa, America & beyond
Spreading the gospel of peace, love, care & trust
The things that we can all feel.

THE LITTLE ONE

The little one is begging
For her mother to give her
This great soft & white ball
So she could bounce it on the lawn
And kick it with her little foot
So that it could roll on the grass;
For her mother to give her
This round & beautiful ball
So that she could hold it to her chest
& spend the whole night hugging it
So to get some love & peace
From this great soft & white ball.

The loving mother regrets this so she says;
We can't give you the ball, my child
This is the moon that hangs in the sky
Without it, the sky is lonely
Without it, the birds are scared
We can't let you cuddle the ball my child
It is the moon that lights the sky
Without it, the world is confused
Without it, all the children are unhappy
So let us sit by the high veranda,
& watch the moon as it goes by.

THE COIN

In the dusty streets I picked a coin
On one side, it was very shiny
As if daily it was being polished
& on this side it was written;
'Peace begins with you,
Peace begins with me;
& peace begins with all of us'

        I looked on the other side
Of this peaceful coin
               It was dull & pale
           As if it was forgotten
    Yet I made great scrutiny…
& on this other side
             It was written;
       'War begins with you,
    War begins with me,
& war begins with all of us'

picked an old book in the library
nd dusted its covers off the dust
hen brought a lantern for illumination
n the first page it was plain
'ith no pictures or shapes drawn
n the bottom of the page it was written

'Love begins with you,
Love begins with me;
& love begins with us of all'

I turned the book to the last cover
On the last page it was written
In gold & curved hand
Like that of a woman in heartbreak
> *Poetry begins with you,*
> *Poetry begins with me,*
> *& poetry begins with all of us'*

THE SILENT WIFE

She doesn't ask me how to dress
But she dresses for me;
She confer with her image in the bedroom mirror,
While I sit reading a newspaper on the bed
But with a sneaking eye watching her;
Once gesturing me to hand over her shoes
Or otherwise to rise & pin up her bra.

She doesn't ask me what to cook
But her cooking is done for me;
In the kitchen, her recipe book she consults
While I sit on a chair playing with my guitar
But watching her with a sore eye
Once waving me to pass her the salt
Or otherwise to hand her a dishtowel.

She doesn't ask me how to love
But her love is meant for me;
She consults her sex magazines
While I lie on the bed pretending to be asleep
But ogle her with an eye, so starved;
Once motioning me to adjust her pillow
Or otherwise pull up the cold and rustling sheets.

IT'S THE POEM

What is it?
That lights the heart
Then catches the eye
And grace the sky
Then kiss the sea
And bless the night
Then hug the hills
No, it is not the moon;
It is the poem.

What is here?
That warms the blood
And light the sky
That brings the life
Then clears the dark
That dries the tears
And brings the flowers
No, it is not the sun;
It is just the poem.

Who goes there?
That sings a song
And sway the trees
Then raise the dust
And sweeps the grass

Then comb the hills
And wave the sea
No. it is not the wind;
It is the bubbly poem.

Who is there?
That moist the eye
And stab the heart
Then freeze the blood
And grip the mind
Then dries the mouth
And stops the breath
No. it is not death
It is the poem

What is it now?
That pumps the blood
And race the heart
Then warm the skin
And wet the lips
Then spin the head
And knocks the senses
Then hold the breath-
No. it is not a kiss alone; it is a poem.

I WILL…..

I will,
Not come around;
But I shall
Not go the round-

I might,
Not love the dark;
But I have
Not known the light.

I may,
Not bring the sun;
But I must
Not bring the moon-

I can,
Not cry again;
But I might
Not laugh aloud.

I would,
Not take a chance;
But I am
Not falling back-

I may,
Not win today;
But I must
Not lose my heart.

I could,
Not force myself;
But I would
Not sit around-

I was,
Not born to rule;
But I might
Not step aside.

I will,
Not stick around;
But I can
Not go away-

I may,
Not cry aloud;
But I have; not cut the pain.

THE BATON

Take this baton
Pass it on
Let it go
Round and round
It's for everyone,
Let everyone have it.
Don't stay long
With the baton
Do not sleep
With the baton
Give it to others;
It's just a baton
Let it move
On and on
Don't get old
With the baton
It's not yours
It's not mine
Let the baton go.
The baton is not,
For men alone;
Let the women have it
The baton must roll
For the good of th' nation,

Pass it on.
Do not die
With the baton
Don't let the baton
Die with you!
Don't be greedy
Pass it on
Everyone is waiting…
For the baton to go
Round and round
Let it change
Hands, everyday.
The baton must go
Let it move
As free and fair.
Do not kill
For the baton
Do not steal
With the baton
Don't be a coward,
Let the baton go
Let the children have it
The baton is for everyone.

THE DIARY OF A SOLDIER

The diary of an American soldier
Or that of a Russian soldier
Be it that of a Liberian soldier
The diary of a soldier;
Is just the same

The diary of a colonel
And the diary of a sergeant
Be it that of a private soldier
The diary of a soldier;
Is just the same story

The diary of a soldier speaks
Of the fear of death
Of his longing for home
Of the memories of his wife & children
Of those waiting for him everyday
It speaks with strength
It speaks sometimes without strength
It speaks vividly of future plans
It relates vividly of good old days
The diary of a soldier is just the same
Be it during peace time or during the war
Is just the same old story.

The diary of a soldier's wife
Is just the same story
Is full of tears
Brief visits and long absences
Is full of fears
Of the horrible news from every knock at the door
Is full of loneliness
It is the same sad story
Of children crying and asking
Of waiting & waiting without knowing
Be it the wife of an Angolan soldier
The fiancé of a French soldier
The bride of a Nigerian officer
The woman of a Zimbabwean gunner;
The diary of a soldier's wife, is just the same.

ORPHANED CHILD

She looked down inside the grave-
Dust falling over the coffin,
& understood;
Her world was falling in that pit
Just in front of her
Her mother was swallowed;
& the earth's hungry mouth was shut.

Her rights were violated
All she had the world had taken
Mother's love
Her fort of confidence
What does the earth gain?
By taking away the one who bathed her;
The one who kissed her forehead.
From today she will not know love
But pity from all that looked in the pit
As the earth swallowed her mother
Without anyone trying to make it stop.

The moment she looked around
Everyone's mother was there
Except her own mother,
& she panicked
As she felt too vulnerable

She wanted to run away
& get home very quickly
Maybe her mother would be there
To let her hold her skirt for safety,
For comfort & for pride.

RESTLESS

I am turning in my bed,
Turning now & then
My wife is turning in her grave,
Turning all the time;
We are both restless.

I try to reach her in my dreams,
To tell her that the children are fine
My voice cannot reach her ears
Besides, her figure is always a shadow.

I try to reach her in my prayers
To tell her that my life is empty
But her deafness is all I get
Besides, there is not enough wind
To carry my prayers far to her ears.

Then I try to hold
In my thoughts & memories
Her figure slipping through my hands
Like a mock shadow made of water
Not really visible, not really tangible;
We are both restless.

SECRETS

The moon has its side so dark
Which it never reveals to the earth,
Nor let the sun's light brighten.
I have known the moon all my life;
In good & in bad times,
Even in rain & in thunder
It has stood with me;
By night it has lit up my paths.
The moon is soft, nice & easy going
But there is one dark secret
Which I don't know about the moon.

The sun visit our village daily
To give us life, warmth and light
And some of us even do worship the sun.
have known the sun since I was a young girl,
fond of sweets, sitting on my father's knee
Now wrinkled & bent, I am advanced in years
But there is one sad secret
That I don't know about the sun;
Why has it vowed to swallow the earth?

Though I have lived
since I was born
for many years now with myself

Today I am ancient and white haired
There is one common secret
Which I don't know about myself;
How can I simply wake up to continue with my life?
In the event that the poisonous arrow of death
Has found its mark on my heart.

But that's not all.
Death is keeping from me its secret
The eagle is keeping his secret from the hen
The lion is guarding his secret from all animals
There are secrets of nations
Secrets of households
Even secrets are there in today's churches.

THE PRESENT AND THE PAST

The past and the present
Have no difference
Because yesterday the past
Has been the present
And tomorrow
The present will be the past.
If the future goes one step backwards
It will be the present
And if it goes another step backwards
It will be the past
If the present steps forward
And all the time steps aside
And the past double steps ahead
It means they have the future with them.

The past and the present
Are like the leaves of a tree
All the fallen leaves are the past
All the hanging leaves are the present
A day gone is a leaf fallen
A fallen leaf is some present sunk in the past
The past and future are one
Because every leaf shall one day fall.

Society might forget the past

And might enjoy the present
Might always plan for the future
But in the end they are all the same.
As everyone tramples on the fallen leaf
But then cherish on the hanging leaf
As there is labour on the future leaf
In the end let it be known
That they shall all decay.

HER LANGUAGE

She is not good at English
She stammers when she tries French
She looks confused when speaking in Shona
She's so bad with her Swahili
But I like her when she speaks in…..
      body-language!

The flutter of her eyes
The bending of her neck
The slight heave of her chest
She speaks in broken vowels
But her silent lips are so fluent
That's how she speaks; in-
      body-language!

    When she walks
  Her whole body speaks volumes
  Of soft & warm words
  Her hand tucks in a stray braid
  Of her long twisted hair
  In a slow & careful way
  I cannot shift my attention
  From her because now she speaks;
    In body-language!

She can say yes
She can laugh & cry
She can show me the way
She can make me happy
She can rule the world
Only by the use of her...
Body-language!

THE SPACE BETWEEN

The space between you & me
Is not good
For the love that we share.
It makes you feel/act like a widow
It is like a sky without the stars
The moon & the sun.
My love; can you forgive me
For creating, or somehow failing to bridge
The space between you & me.

The space between the children & myself
Is not empty
But full of their voices in agony
Ever begging me to come home
Always worried for me every night
Their patience is not going to take it any more
For they do not understand
The power of the space between
& what makes me fail to come home tonight

The space between us
Is divided by rivers & mountains
Is like I am dead, you alive/vice versa
The space between, has turned my hair white &
deeper than the sea-

Is hungrier than the sea-
So I cannot come home
Until the tide has lowered down surely

The space between us all
Is so devastating
Hence it's empty of happiness
Yet it is not quiet at all
But full of restless dreams
& filled with stabbing memories
The space;
Is measured in crawling days & weeks
Is just timeless/darkness, yes; timeless over darkness
Yet it has given me time to think
Of all the good things that I am missing
The space between us all
Has inflicted me with high blood pressure
And given me so much to think of.

HER PAPERS

The fire in her eyes
Sets like the western sun
Her struggling to breathe,
Like some candle in a vacuum
Something dark is embracing her;
Something light is letting her go.
It's not kind of a wrestling,
But you could see negotiations are taking place,
Between light and darkness
They will not leave the table
Until the papers are signed & stamped;
To be approved with a white & a dark stamp
Her name written everywhere
Signatures in dark and light scribbled
Envelopes sealed (with tight signets)
Waiting for the mail cart
In the far distance
The steel wheels scuttling
Drawing closer & louder;
The horse beats drumming
Time long past midnight
They will not leave the table
Until all papers are cleared
But they fear will meet the twilight,
Before her papers are done.

Her papers;
Maybe they are not clean
Maybe they are not complete
Suddenly came from the east;
A swift chariot of fire
That overtook the scuttling mail cart
As surprisingly;
The fire in her eyes
Began to rekindle;
And to kindle
Like the sun in the East;
The twilight had struck her brows.

EMMA THE JEWISH GIRL [2]

She is slim

Like a Muslim;

She is elite

Like an Israelite;

She has traces

Of many, many races.

Her bum;

As huge as an album.

The blue eyed Emma

Has put me at a dilemma.

She has black knees,

Like those of a Sudanese.

For my love to be legal

I wish;

I was Jewish.

THE NEW CONVERT'S MIND

Death! Death! Death!
Death cannot separate us apart
Maybe our flesh, but not our souls.

What is heaven to me?
If I go there without my wife
What is the paradise to me?
When my children are crying in hell.
I'd rather be with them in flames
Than to sit in heaven & be of good cheer.

Are they not the ones I had struggled for?
Sacrificing my life; Sweating & toiling.
I pledge my sacrifices even beyond this earth
How can I rejoice with strangers in heaven?
When my mother is being roasted by great flames.

Heaven must be entered as a family
My parents my siblings my friends
Otherwise how can I be eating?
With someone who rejected my own child
& throw him to the wrath of hell.
It is my young son's happiness I desire first
What I want first is my little daughter's safety
All that is important is the welfare of my wife

Even heaven isn't good for me without them.

CAN WE?

Can we actually run
From what the bible says?
& at the end of times
Be victorious of the whole race.
If we can actually twist
That which the bible paints
Can we also twist?
Our way inside the gates of heaven.
Those who actually ignore
All that the bible shares
Are they going to remain?
When the time for them comes
To make a foundation for their own life.
Can we actually manipulate?
The path that the moon follow
And the way that the sun shine
And the season that the rains fall
And at the end of times
Reset the dials of what we had tampered with.
Can we actually understand?
What the bible says
If we rely on interpretations
That are founded by people
Who are so mean as to personalise
The single Father that all lives have to share.

CROSSING

The old have crossed
The young are crossing
& the youngest have not crossed.
Those who die
Are the youngest
That cross before their time.

The old have said it
The young are saying it
& the youngest will say it.
Those we praise,
Are the old
Because they have already said it.

The old have fought it
With bows, spears & arrows
The young are fighting it
With guns, warplanes & nuclear
& the youngest have not fought it yet.
Those who have fresh scars
Are the young
Because they are fighting it now.

MY CHILDHOOD

(1)
Childhood was never time to cry;
Back then i used to sing
From my mother's back
When i felt the beat, pulse
Plus the rhythm
Of her body from the outside.

(2)
I used to coo from her back
Inspired by the musical chords
Piped by the wind;
Coming from the hills, &
Coming through the trees,
Across from the Nyajezi River.

3)
Childhood was never time to lack;
 used to sing
'rom my mother's breast;
timulated by heavy drumbeats
)f her gracious heart,
ast & slow drumming
gainst my small attentive ear.

TONIGHT

Tonight I will be going down to the beach
Because there is a full moon tonight
I will walk about with my small feet;
My feet will be bare & warm
Will be warmed by the fine sand
Which the departed sun had radiated
& my hands will be warm
Will be warmed by my mom & dad
Fondly holding my little palms
As we walk down the sandy beach.

My eyes will be warm as a lamb
Warmed by the misty glow of the moon;
Pure & fluorescent without any rays
My young heart will be warmer than ever
Warmed by the love of my caring parents
Protecting me so well like heavenly angels
As I walk about with my small feet
My face is so warm tonight
Warmed by the breeze & wheezing
From the sea, tonight
I will be going down to the beach.

Tonight I will be counting the stars
Because the moon is full & bright

And the sky is clear & near
Reflecting in the calm sea
Tonight I will be grouping the stars
According to their sizes
& arranging them by their types
Tonight I will be rearranging the stars
As per their sex & by their names
I will be counting them all the stars
By their race & nationality
At the beach
Where the sky is clear
And the moon is bright
And the sea is calm & clear
I will be counting all the stars
Until the sun comes up in the morning.

WE HAVE

We have wept much
More than the heavy rainy clouds
For the things that's out of our reach
For things that are of little use
Yet our tears never watered a single seed,
We have wept much;
Because we are people.
We have complained much
More than the bare mountains
That have seen it all
From the time the world was born,
We are forever mumbling;
Because we are human beings.
We have boasted, much
More than the silent moon
That we know everything;
Isn't it yesterday that we were born?
Challenging the moon born with the world,
We think we know everything
Because we are people.

THE LIMIT

To the living
The sky, is the limit
Yet it is limitless
But to the dead
The grave is the limit;
Yes it is limited.

To the living, gravity
Is a troublesome force
That binds them down
From crowding in the sky
That we all believe
To be the limit.
In such a way
The dead are locked
In the limit of the grave
& are the ones that have realised
If death wasn't an infringement
Of a couple of some rights;
Life & death would be the same.
Or a life cycle itself from life to death
From the sky limit to the grave limit.

SENTIMENTS

I have some true sentiments
That tomorrow the weather will be too cold
Because of the deep operation in my belly

I have some sentiments
That tomorrow the rains will truly fall
Because of the asthma in my bones

With this infirmity
Society does benefit from it
Through my suffering & great pain

I have some correct sentiments
That the moon is now young in the sky
Now because my mentally ill brother John
Is getting more violent & really confused

With this his suffering
We are able to follow the seasons
& to mark our traditional calendar
Such that time is not lost to us

I have some definite sentiments
That the trees are flowering again
I hear my mother coughing strangely

Red are her eyes & her skin swelling
Because of her allergy in flowering plants.

THE GARDEN

Her heart is the garden

Of roses & blooming flowers

That I tend every year & season

By keeping the snow away

& regulate the shining sun.

I prune the roses, I water them too

I weed, I care all the year round;
That is how a woman's heart is cared for.

The mistake of my life!

Was to cut a blooming flower with my shears

Down it tumbled, and suddenly I recalled her words;

'Don't ever cut a rose from my heart's garden!'

The fallen flower turned into a butterfly

That flew & settle on each and every standing rose

Its poisonous kiss turning all the flowers into butterflies

They shook their bright wings; testing the wind

& then flew out into the unknown world;

Leaving the garden dull & without a scent
& I knew I had lost her heart forever.

THE POETRY BEAR

The hunters are gathered, all are together
They bring their advanced skills,
To be employed in the hills
Safety is the motto for today they are hunting.
They come in different units,
They bring various weapons
Some from the East & some from the West
Now they are geared up for hunting;
Hunting down the poetry bear.
It is a brown bear they are hunting,
For innumerable days following its spoor
Trailing it here; trailing it there; trailing it here & there
The hunters are hunting down the poetry bear
They locate it in low elevations of the river valley
Hunting moose & foraging up & down;
The poetry bear is hunting
It is waiting for the salmon to come; waiting & waiting
Now it fights as it is cornered
By spears & arrows; it counterattacks.
It shook its fur, it bares its teeth
It roars like a lion; fighting its battles
For how long will it continue fighting?
Because the hunters are pressing it hard & fast
They are shooting it from a tree-stand,
Zeroing at its front shoulder

With the muzzle-loader exploding,
The huntsmen firing & firing
They strike they fire they shoot without ceasing
It is a brawny brown poetry bear,
With resilience & endurance, it is tough.
Until nightfall it continue to fight,
Then vanishes into the close darkness
The hunters are gathered again,
To track down the strong poetry bear
It is a grizzly bear they are hunting in the high country
The poetry bear foraging peacefully in summer
Foraging up, foraging down; foraging up & down
For how long will they search?
They found it on the rock faces now;
The hunters are strong, the hunters
Are fit; they are strong & fit.
With hounds they chase it in rounds
They chase it for hours, they chase
t for ages; they pursue it for miles.
'or how long will it run & run, for how long will it flee?
he poetry bear is being driven to tiredness
he hunters are being driven to madness
he hunters are closing-in; equipped
With rifles & pitchforks, they are deadly.
hey have catapults, they have axes they have knobkerries
o pelt & hew & smash the poetry bear
lie low in the trees, it hides in the snow,
takes cover in the holes it hides everywhere

It hides without luck, it hides
Without success; it hides without luck & success
It is a sturdy poetry bear it outruns them in the woods
& for many months the hunters are hunting up & down
They have stretched bows & poisoned
Arrows, hunting far, hunting wide;
Hunting far & wide; hunting down the bear of poetry.
They set snare traps for it everywhere,
So the poetry bear they may capture
They dig trap-holes
They set toils of nets in its pathways
In the river valley in the high country, traps
Are set in the hills & game areas.
When is it that they will locate the poetry bear again?
The hunt units are everywhere camping;
Camping up, camping down; camping up and down
Consulting the topographical map for his whereabouts
Imitating wounded animal calls by day & by night;
They call by day & night
The poetry bear hunters; it is a black bear they are hunting
When will he finally come out?
The hunters are wondering day & night
The poetry bear is hiding away; hiding, hiding
He can hear the smell of burnt sugar
& the lard baits are everywhere
But he cannot come out for he is wondering....
Is it the meat they want, is it the coat he wears?
Is it true its teeth & claws?

Are used for the charms they wear
He is wondering, he is in hiding;
Hiding & wondering the poetry bear hiding.

WHEN THE PARTY BEGIN

When the fighting begun

Everyone was holding a gun

When the party begin

Everyone was holding a gin

When the party end

Everyone had a friend

But the fighting never did end

& nobody was a friend.

We do not hold a gin

When the fighting begin

& we don't hold a gun

When the party has begun.

Life gives us back

What we give to life

If we give it a gun;

It gives back to us a fight

& if we give it a gin;

From life we get a party.

DELIGHT

They sat on a mat;
Her odour is salty and raw,
& as ironical as hot iron.
In beauty & virtue
She was rather rich than poor
He touched her wet lips
Their drift has no rift-
Like a dream, a nice dream.

Shiny roubles glittering in her eyes,
Are the heart's signs of no worrying
This is the time for him
To be closest to her;
& make her feel more important,
Above everything he has in his life.

So sure is she now
He isn't like a pretending serpent
Which was found in the church
& said I have come to repent.
Her heart is beating and repeating;
Her blood is just getting settled,
As he carefully continue soothing her nerves.

This is time,
To plead their interdependence

This is time,
To communicate by the eyes only;
Maybe with a gentle touch of fingertips.
Such this love they have found
Will never fade or get lost.

SPRING

Now is the coming of time of spring
The forest & the wind huddled, whisp'ring
The trees are almost leafless
& the leaves dropped on the ground, lifeless
The cooing of a peaceful dove brings
A feeling that is sob'ring
The bees are passing in a string
To mate those flowers that are ready for pest'ring.

Spring is a forest straggling
With new nature sprouting & struggling
It is too soon all the old brown glades
Will be getting new green blades
As many as the colourful flowers in their windings
The flies are on the quest for their findings

Spring brings strings of the awakening of clover
& the revisiting of the long gone plover
In its tranquil hours cries the bittern
The humming wasps had every flower sucked & bitten
Just underneath, the earth is in a great motivation
As nature makes wonders of its own cultivation
Which suddenly explodes into an overwhelming springtime
That every animal comes to enjoy the abundance;
Springtime is a time for joy & dance
The season that God bless
Is a time for everyone's bliss.

THE RAPT SENSES

The sun stopped

& listened to the moon

No. but it is the wind

That is whispering.

Are they the stars?

That are winking,

Or it is my eyes;

That are blinking?

The moon is cold;

: is dead.

he sun is warming life into it,

the rain soaks life into it;

Then the wind breathes life into it.

Full of life, full of energy;

The sun is sweating hard

But it cannot awaken the moon.

Blinking and winking;

My eyes and stars are watching.

THE LION KING

I am a flower
Born with thorns
As sharp as claws,
Of the lion king

Am a pretty flower
Living with poison
Flowing in my veins
Lacing my petals
Deadly as the venom,
Of the viper king

I do not believe in
Baring my fangs
Out In the jungle world,
As the lion king

Can't bring myself to
Slither around the night
Sticking poisonous lips
Causing painful deaths,
Like the viper king

Am a pretty flower
In a pretty vase

Among the innocent children
Cared for by the maidens
No-body understands why,
I'm the lion king.

SENTIMENTS OF THE EARTH

The mother of all nations is crying
Shedding black tears of death
From the coughing of some sick nations
Spreading a deadly cold and flu
That paralyses her lungs and airways
The nations are coughing toxic fumes
In the air and rivers and on the ground
The mother of all nations is smarting
From the smoke of speeding automobiles
And the gusts billowing all hours of the week
From the giant industries of nations
And soon she is getting blind without our expertise
To bring her back her eyesight to life
The mother of all nations is suffocating
The trees she uses as breathing nostrils
Are being cut everyday by all nations
As they feed them in their giant timber companies
The mother of nations is failing to make the rains
Because her cauldrons are being disturbed
By the acts of some nations making nuclear bombs
When her temperature suddenly rises
She is like a woman just missing her period
Yet there is nothing growing in her womb
The mother of all nations is groaning
From the daily all nations activities

As they play with greenhouse gases
Burning coal, oil and gas
On her endangered lungs& breathing space
Yet for the sake of our own
Continues to circle the tormenting sun
In her induced nakedness
Splashing the waves of the seas
Shedding salty tears of pain.

FLOWERS EVERYWHERE

Flowers for the newly dead
Flowers on the tombstone head
Flowers for the newly weds
Flowers at the wedding
Flowers in the sunshine, rain & the dark
Flowers in the rivers, blooming for the toads
Flowers of the deserts
Flowers in the marsh lands
Flowers through the winter, flowers every season
Flowers for the girls, flowers in their dreams
Flowers & the honey bees
Flowers in the morning
Flowers & the joyful birds
Flowers within the bright moon
Flowers against the bright stars
Flowers everywhere
Flowers for the comfort, flowers for the love
Happy flowers, gloomy flowers making up the day
Flowers in the dark bush, where the lion sleeps
Flowers on the book cover, or the surface of the earth
Flowers in the wind, clinging to the ground
Flowers on the draw board, breathing without life
Flowers as a medicine, taken to be herbs
Flowers of the greenhouse
Flowers by the nature, flowers & the finches

Flowers of the wild, flowers along the river bank
Flowers on the extinction, flowers of the flower pot
Flowers for the happy, flowers for the hurt
Flowers without flowers
Flowers unlike flowers
Flowers as in flowers, flowers are flowers.

MY SKIN SPEAKS

I the skin, I am not a sin
Whether in yellow, white & black
My colour is not traffic lights:
Black: STOP
White: GO
Yellow: PREPARE TO GO;
Red, green & amber style.

My nature is not painted sky-lines;
Black: DUSK
White: DAWN
Yellow: NOWHERE;
Red, green & amber style.

My hue is not some garden earth;
White: FERTILE
Black: BARREN
Yellow: EMPTY.
We can all be fertile
And we must all see the dawn;
We were all created to: GO.

AWAKENED

Life & fire breathed
Into the Abrahamic idols
African wooden & pottery images
Awake from their slumbers
To take charge of the pulpit.

AFRICAN POETRY

It all comes from within
The villages of their birth
Their poetry falls from high up the palm trees
They squeeze it out like some fruit juice
They winnow it off in the open wind
With reed baskets tilted to the windward
They pound it like the yams
For the whole day with pestle & mortar
By women wrapped in colourful attires
They mill it on smooth rocks like millet meal
And crush it for the juice like oranges
Filling clay pots as warm as cellars
Of the potent & hearty ancestral drink.

This has always been the land
Of their fathers & ancestors
Their poetry is harvested from the farmlands
Where they toiled with hoes & machetes
Beneath the rich earth that they turn
With ox-drawn ploughs to show a new beginning
Of a fruitful season in their remote village.

They speak not of hunger
In the village life isn't a cry
Their poetry comes from the kitchen hut

At the hearth where their food is cooked
Where they all gather at the fireplace
For warmth & storytelling nights
While the yellow flames burn out from hard logs
Cremated into clear white ash
Concealing red hot ambers that would hibernate
Until the following morning to begin a new day.

Their poetry comes from the wombs
Of their wives & mothers & sisters
They push it out like delivering mothers
Or cut it out like the caesarean midwife
And the poetry comes out shrieking like babies
They live in great harmony
With the culture of their land
That is marked with strange provisions
Witnessed by the first missionaries from overseas.
They sneeze it out like a cat;
Throughout the day their poetry speaks.

HER RAINBOW SONG BOOK

She took the colour of the sunset
And mix with the thickness of rain clouds
She pours a breeze from the south wind
And from a mixture of these;
She moulds a holocaust poetry verse.

She cut the early flowers at sunrise
Then paused on the icy mountain top
To sketch the faraway sea, the desert & the great forests
With the yellowish sun slanting westward
She came down smiling;
All dimples, snowflakes, a smoking breath;
Now to write a homely poetry book.

She smeared the clear sky with some paint
And cut off a slice from the pale moon
She shook the stars in a silver vial
To make some bubbles in the sky
Then poured the milk upon the darkly sky
As she hang out everything to dry
She sat down on a small wooden stool
To write a remarkable poetry vision.

She let him come closely up
To hold her hand & whisper a word

And promise her a marriage when his fortune is ripe
She let a bee settle on her nose
To lick her dewed early morning sweat
And promise her some honey when the table is set
She let the wind tap her eyes
To bring out rolling tears of angels
That fires her icy cheeks & tickle her skin
To bring a wide smile from the candy lips
She could hear her heart pumping up & up;
Like to the beat of a poetry song.

I AM IN LOVE

I am in love
I have love
There is true love swelling in my heart;
If I give it to the sun
One day the clouds will come over it
To hide the sun away from my presence
And I will be left alone to cry.

I am with love
I have some love
There is too much love boiling in my heart;
If I extend it to some colourful flower
One day a worm will come and burrow inside it
And its green leaves will wilt away;
All those bright petals falling one by one
And I will be left with nothing but bare twigs.

I must love
I have love to share
There is love burning inside me;
If I give it to the mountains
One day the snow will come and cover it
From its summit down to the bottom
And I would be left to freeze
My heart for the entire days of winter time.

I can love
I have love
There is love tingling in my blood;
If I give it to this cute guy
One day a ravishing girl will take him away
And I would be left alone to grieve and nursing
A broken heart and wounds in tears.

I have some love
I have got love
There is passionate love in my heart;
If I surrender it up to the sea
One day a storm will come over
And the floods will wash me away
And thereafter thrown up on some rugged rocks
Leaving me almost dead and half buried
While it rages on and on in its ungentle love.

I have true love
I feel some love
There is abundant love in my heart;
If I give it to Jesus Christ
One day he will take me with him
Through the sky without the use of ladders
To his father's house where he lives.

Printed in the United States
By Bookmasters